Tex

Extremely Good Clean Jokes for Kids

Bob Phillips

Harvest House Publishers
Eugene, Oregon 97402

EXTREMELY GOOD CLEAN JOKES FOR KIDS
Copyright © 2001 Bob Phillips
Published by Harvest House Publishers
Eugene, Oregon 97402

ISBN: 0-7369-0309-7

Printed in the United States of America.

01 02 03 04 05 06 / BC-MS / 10 9 8 7 6 5 4

To
Owen East Anderson—
who loves to laugh.

Contents

1

Argyle and Angus

Argyle: What is a good way to kill time in the winter?
Angus: Search me.
Argyle: Sleigh it.

Argyle: What is the difference between a cat and a bullfrog?
Angus: Beats me.
Argyle: The cat has nine lives, but the bullfrog croaks every night.

Argyle: What is big enough to hold a pig and small enough to hold in your hands?
Angus: My mind is a blank.
Argyle: A pen.

8

Argyle: What is the best name for the wife of a
    lawyer?
Angus: I'm in the dark.
Argyle: Sue.

Argyle: What is the best name for the wife of a
    jeweler?
Angus: I don't have the foggiest.
Argyle: Ruby.

Argyle: What is the difference between progress
    and Congress?
Angus: I'm blank.
Argyle: Pro and con.

Argyle: What time is it when you see a monkey
    scratching for a flea with his left hand?
Angus: That's a mystery.
Argyle: Five after one.

Argyle: What did one shrub say to the other?
Angus: I have no idea.
Argyle: Boy, am I bushed.

Argyle: What has four legs and flies?
Angus: I don't know.
Argyle: A horse.

Argyle: What kind of servants are best for hotels?
Angus: I pass.
Argyle: The inn-experienced.

Argyle: What is the best name for the wife of a
civil engineer?
Angus: Who knows?
Argyle: Bridget.

Argyle: What is appropriate material for a
dairyman to wear?
Angus: I give up.
Argyle: Cheesecloth.

Argyle: What did one watch say to another?
Angus: You tell me.
Argyle: Hour you doing?

Argyle: What did one arithmetic book say to the
other?
Angus: I have no clue.
Argyle: I've got problems.

Argyle: What letter is nine inches long?
Angus: I can't guess.
Argyle: The letter Y; it is one-fourth of a yard.

Argyle: What is always coming but never arrives?
Angus: Search me.
Argyle: Tomorrow.

Argyle: What do you call a boomerang that doesn't
    come back?
Angus: I'm in the dark.
Argyle: A stick.

★ ★ ★

Argyle: What beverage is appropriate for a golfer?
Angus: I don't have the foggiest.
Argyle: Tea.

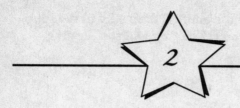

Waiter, Waiter!

Customer: Waiter, waiter! I don't like the flies in here.
Waiter: Well, come back tomorrow. We'll have new ones by then!

Customer: Waiter, waiter! Bring me something to eat and make it snappy.
Waiter: How about a crocodile sandwich, sir?

Customer: What's this in my soup?
Waiter: I don't know, sir, all insects look the same to me.

★ ★ ★

Customer: Waiter, Waiter! Do you have frog's legs?
Waiter: No, ma'am, it's just the way I'm standing.

Customer: Waiter, Waiter! There's a fly in my soup.
Waiter: Don't worry! The frog will surface any
minute.

Customer: What's that?
Waiter: It's a tomato surprise.
Customer: I can't see any tomatoes in it.
Waiter: I know, sir. That's the surprise.

Customer: Waiter, waiter! There's a small slug in
my salad!
Waiter: I do apologize, sir. Would you like a bigger
one?

Customer: Waiter, waiter! What's wrong with this
fish?
Waiter: Long time no sea, sir.

Customer: Waiter, there are 49 flies in my soup.
Waiter: One more and we'll beat the world record!

Customer: Waiter, waiter! This soup tastes funny.
Waiter: Then why aren't you laughing?

Customer: Waiter, waiter! There's a dead beetle in my gravy.
Waiter: Yes, sir. Beetles are terrible swimmers.

Customer: Waiter, I can't find one clam in this clam chowder!
Waiter: Oh, and I suppose you expect to find angels in your angel food cake, too!

Customer: Waiter, I don't see any chocolate cake on this menu.
Waiter: No, sir. I wiped it off.

Customer: Waiter, what is this dish?
Waiter: It's bean soup, sir.
Customer: Yes, but what is it now?

Customer: Waiter, there is a button in my soup.
Waiter: Thank goodness for that! I've been looking for it everywhere.

★ ★ ★

Customer: Waiter, these eggs are runny.
Waiter: Why do you say that?
Customer: Because one just ran out the door.

Knock, Knock!

Knock, knock
Who's there?
Colleen.
Colleen who?
Colleen yourself up, you're a mess!

Knock, knock
Who's there?
Delphis.
Delphis who?
Delphis fine, thanks.

Knock, knock.
Who's there?
Soup.
Soup who?
Souper Man!

★ ★ ★

Knock, knock.
Who's there?
Bolivia.
Bolivia who?
Bolivia me, I know what I'm talking about.

★ ★ ★

Knock, knock.
Who's there?
Juanita.
Juanita who?
Juanita big meal?

★ ★ ★

Knock, knock.
Who's there?
Pasture.
Pasture who?
Pasture bedtime. Go to sleep.

★ ★ ★

Knock, knock.
Who's there?
June.
June who?
June know how to open a door?

★ ★ ★

Knock, knock.
Who's there?

Megan.
Megan who?
Megan a loud noise.

★ ★ ★

Knock, knock.
Who's there?
Attilla.
Attilla who?
Attilla you no lies, it's really me.

★ ★ ★

Knock, knock.
Who's there?
Elizabeth.
Elizabeth who?
Elizabeth of knowledge is a dangerous thing.

★ ★ ★

Knock, knock.
Who's there?
Robin.
Robin who?
Robin you, so hand over your money!

★ ★ ★

Knock, knock.
Who's there?
Eve.
Eve who?
Eve-ho, here we go.

Knock, knock.
Who's there?
Eileen.
Eileen who?
Eileen Dover and fell off my chair!

Knock, knock.
Who's there?
Alma.
Alma who?
Almany times do I have to knock?

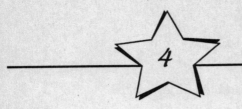

Basil and Baxter

Basil: What can fill a whole house and still weigh
less than a tiny mouse?
Baxter: Search me.
Basil: Smoke.

Basil: What is nothing but holes tied to holes; yet is
as strong as steel?
Baxter: I'm in the dark.
Basil: A chain.

Basil: What did one pig say to another?
Baxter: I don't have the foggiest.
Basil: I'll give you lots of hogs and kisses.

Basil: What did the bull say to the cow?
Baxter: I'm blank.
Basil: When I fall in love, it will be for heifer.

Basil: What do you get if you cross a lizard with a
   baseball player?
Baxter: That's a mystery.
Basil: An outfielder who catches flies on his tongue
   and eats them.

Basil: What would you get if you crossed Prince
   Charles with Moby Dick?
Baxter: I have no idea.
Basil: The Prince of Whales.

Basil: What would you get if you crossed a dog
   with a cartoon sailor?
Baxter: I don't know.
Basil: Pupeye!

Basil: What two letters of the alphabet do children
   like best?
Baxter: I pass.
Basil: C and Y.

Basil: What would you get if you crossed a radio commentator with a cheese?
Baxter: Beats me.
Basil: Rush Limburger.

Basil: What hand do you use to stir your cocoa?
Baxter: My mind is a blank.
Basil: I always use a spoon, myself.

Basil: What do you feed your pet frog?
Baxter: Who knows?
Basil: Croakers and milk!

Basil: What always has its eye open, but never sees anything?
Baxter: I give up.
Basil: A needle.

Basil: What is an important aid for pet mice with bad breath?
Baxter: You tell me.
Basil: Mousewash!

Basil: What's so fragile you can break it with a whisper?

Baxter: I have no clue.
Basil: A secret.

Basil: What's the difference between a cat and a
hockey puck?
Baxter: I can't guess.
Basil: About two IQ points.

Basil: What's red-and-white-and-blue all over?
Baxter: Search me.
Basil: A candy cane holding its breath!

Basil: What do you get if you cross a rattlesnake
with a doughnut?
Baxter: I'm in the dark.
Basil: A snake that rattles and rolls.

Basil: What country do cows love to visit?
Baxter: I don't have the foggiest.
Basil: Moo Zealand!

Side Splitters

I hate housework. You make the beds, you do the dishes, and six months later you have to start all over again.

We had such a bad team that every time we took the field our manager got fined for littering.

Love makes the world go 'round, but laughter keeps us all from jumping off.

They asked my Uncle Ambrose if anybody in his family suffers from insanity. He said, "No, they all seem to be enjoying it."

We were losing one game 76 to 0, but we weren't worried. We hadn't had our turn at bat yet.

I once prayed in a hotel, and they charged me a 75-cent long distance charge.

Did you hear about the newlyweds who were so frail that they got knocked out cold when their friends threw rice at them?

Show me a guy who plays basketball in a tuxedo, and I'll show you a gym dandy.

I read in a newspaper about a kangaroo in the San Diego Zoo that has no pep. The vet diagnosed him as out of bounds.

A chemist driving to the lab happened to see a car run over a rabbit. He stopped, got out of his car, and revived the rabbit with smelling salts. A bystander said, "What did you use to make that rabbit hop away?" The chemist grinned and said, "Hare restorer."

24

Did you hear about the goat who swallowed the rabbit who became the hare in the butter?

The teacher in the school for pigeons had just about given up on one of her pupils.

"Either you fly tomorrow, or I'll put a rope on you and tow you around," she said.

"Oh, don't do that!" he said. "I don't want to be pigeon-toed."

A man went into the local department store where he saw a sign on the escalator: "Dogs must be carried on this escalator." The silly man then spent the next two hours looking for a dog.

Three little boys were bragging about how tough they were.

"I wear out a pair of shoes in a month," the first little boy said.

"I wear out a pair of jeans in a week," the second little boy said.

"That's nothing," the other little boy said. "I wear out a babysitter in 20 minutes."

Today's cars are aerodynamically designed. They're built to sit in traffic jams at high speed.

Did You Hear?

Did you hear the one about the tornado? It will blow you away!

Did you hear the one about the cookie? It's crumby!

Did you hear about the woman who had a weird accident? She fell asleep while knitting, poked a hole in her waterbed, and drowned.

Did you ever hear the story of the new roof? It's over your head.

Did you hear about the skunk who had no nose? He smelled terrible.

Did you hear about the restless sleeper who bought a waterbed?
He tossed and turned so much that he made himself seasick.

Did you hear the one about the dynamite? It's a blast!

Did you hear the one about the snake? It's hissterical!

Did you hear the one about the owl? It's a hoot!

Did you hear the one about the redwood? It's treemendous!

Did you hear the one about the Milky Way? It's out of this world!

Did you hear the one about the electric drill? It's boring!

Did you hear the one about the ruby? It's a real gem!

Did you hear the one about the Mississippi River? It's all wet!

Did you hear the one about amnesia? You'll probably forget it.

Did you hear the one about the clouds? It's over your head!

Did you hear the one about the helium balloon? It's a gas!

Did you hear the one about the broken pencil? It's pointless!

Did you hear the one about the air conditioner? It's so cool!

Did you hear the one about the electric eel? It's shocking!

Clairbelle and Clayborne

Clairbelle: What has 50 heads but can't think?
Clayborne: I'm in the dark.
Clairbelle: A box of matches.

Clairbelle: What three noblemen are mentioned in
the Bible?
Clayborne: I don't have the foggiest.
Clairbelle: Barren fig tree, Lord how long, and
Count thy blessings.

Clairbelle: What has a head like a cat, feet like a
cat, a tail like a cat, but isn't a cat?
Clayborne: That's a mystery.
Clairbelle: A kitten.

Clairbelle: Which clothes last the longest?
Clayborne: I have no idea.
Clairbelle: Pajamas, for they are never worn out.

Clairbelle: What is appropriate material for a
filling station operator to wear?
Clayborne: I don't know.
Clairbelle: Oilcloth.

Clairbelle: What do you call a golf ball after you
hit it?
Clayborne: I pass.
Clairbelle: Lost.

Clairbelle: What would you get if you crossed an
idiot weirdo with a famous college football
team?
Clayborne: Beats me.
Clairbelle: Notre Dumb!

Clairbelle: What pine has the longest and sharpest
needles?
Clayborne: My mind is a blank.
Clairbelle: A porcupine.

Clairbelle: What beverage represents the beginning of time?
Clayborne: Who knows?
Clairbelle: T.

Clairbelle: What is the best name for the wife of a doctor?
Clayborne: I give up.
Clairbelle: Patience.

Clairbelle: What is appropriate material for a fisherman to wear?
Clayborne: You tell me.
Clairbelle: Fishnet.

Clairbelle: What do people in Colorado call little gray cats?
Clayborne: I have no clue.
Clairbelle: Kittens.

★ ★ ★

Clairbelle: What kind of jam cannot be eaten?
Clayborne: I can't guess.
Clairbelle: A traffic jam.

★ ★ ★

Clairbelle: What would you say if I asked you out?
Clayborne: Nothing! I can't talk and gag at the same time.

Clairbelle: What beverage is appropriate for a prize fighter?
Clayborne: I'm in the dark.
Clayborne: Punch.

Clairbelle: What suit lasts longer than you want it to?
Clayborne: I don't have the foggiest.
Clairbelle: A lawsuit.

★ ★ ★

Clairbelle: What is the most dangerous animal in the yard?
Clayborne: I'm blank.
Clairbelle: A clotheslion

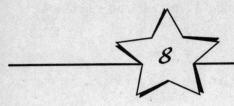

School Daze

Teacher: Name the four seasons.
Student: Football, basketball, baseball, and soccer.

Teacher: Sally, I was just reading over this letter you did. Your inputting is really improving. I see there are only seven mistakes here.
Student: Thank you!
Teacher: Now, let's take a look at the second line.

Teacher: If you stood with your back to the north and faced due south, what would be on your left hand?
Student: Fingers.

Emily: My geometry teacher lost her parrot.
Lacey: How did you find that out?
Emily: When I asked, "Where's your polygon?"

Teacher: What do you get if you add 8,136 and
7,257, subtract 93, and divide the answer by 5?
Tyler: A headache.

Teacher: Does anyone have a garbage disposal unit
at home?
Student: Yes, ma'am, we have one, but it isn't in
the house.
Teacher: Then where is it?
Student: Out in the pigpen.

Teacher: Tell me about the Iron Age.
Student: Sorry, I'm a little rusty on that subject.

Teacher: If I had ten oranges in one hand and six in
the other, what would I have?
Student: Big hands.

Teacher: A job well done need not be done again.
Student: What about mowing the lawn?

Teacher: If you insist on talking, I'll have to send you to the principal's office.

Student: Oh, does the principal need somebody to talk to?

★ ★ ★

A letter sent home by a teacher: "Lester is trying—very."

★ ★ ★

Teacher: Name four animals that belong to the cat family.

Student: The mama cat, the papa cat, and two kittens.

★ ★ ★

Student: I don't have a pencil to take this exam.

Teacher: What would you think of a soldier who went into battle without a gun?

Student: I'd think he was an officer.

★ ★ ★

Teacher: Did you reprimand your little boy for mimicking me?

Parent: Yes, I told him not to act like a fool.

★ ★ ★

Teacher: If you had three apples and ate one, how many would you have?

Student: Three.

Teacher: Three?
Student: Yes. Two outside and one inside.

Teacher: If I lay one egg on this chair and two on the table, how many will I have altogether?
Student: Personally, I don't believe you can do it.

Teacher: Birds, though small, are remarkable creatures. For example, what can a bird do that I can't do?
Student: Take a bath in a saucer.

Teacher: If you had five pieces of candy, and Joey asked you for one, how many pieces would you have left?
Student: Five.

Teacher: This is the fifth day this week you're late! What do you have to say for yourself?
Student: I'm sure glad it's Friday.

Teacher: How would you treat a pig that's been stung by a bee?
Student: Apply oinkment.

Teacher: Are there any unusual children in your class?

Student: Yes, three of them have good manners.

Student to mother: "The principal thinks I am very responsible. Every time something goes wrong at school, he says I am responsible."

Teacher: Give me a sentence with the word "Camelot" in it.

Student: Right, teacher. A camelot is a place where the Arabs park their camels!

Teacher: There will be only a half day of school this morning.

Students: Whoopee! Hooray!

Teacher: We'll have the other half this afternoon.

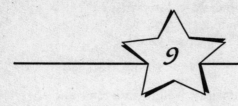

Desmond and Dempsey

Desmond: What's red, white, blue, and green?
Dempsey: Search me.
Desmond: A patriotic pickle!

★ ★ ★

Desmond: What brand of diapers do mother cats
    prefer?
Dempsey: I'm in the dark.
Desmond: Pam-purrs.

★ ★ ★

Desmond: What did the cowboy yell to the sailor
    who was stuck out on the lake?
Dempsey: I don't have the foggiest.
Desmond: Hey, pardner! Whoa, whoa, whoa your
    boat.

★ ★ ★

Desmond: What do you get if you cross a parrot with a huge emerald-colored man?
Dempsey: I'm blank.
Desmond: The Polly Green Giant.

Desmond: What's gray, weighs five tons, and bounces?
Dempsey: That's a mystery.
Desmond: An elephant bungee jumping.

Desmond: What is big, round, and acts crazy?
Dempsey: I have no idea.
Desmond: A fool moon.

Desmond: What do they call a chicken inspector?
Dempsey: I don't know.
Desmond: A cluck watcher.

Desmond: What has big arms, eats spinach, and sells mobile homes?
Dempsey: I pass.
Desmond: Popeye the Trailer Man.

★ ★ ★

Desmond: What's big and purple and hugs your Easter basket?

Dempsey: Beats me.
Desmond: The Easter Barney!

Desmond: What made the cow jump over the
 moon?
Dempsey: My mind is a blank.
Desmond: The milkmaid had cold hands.

Desmond: What's big, gray, very heavy, and wears
 glass slippers?
Dempsey: Who knows?
Desmond: Cinderellaphant.

Desmond: What is a dolphin's favorite TV show?
Dempsey: I give up.
Desmond: Whale of Fortune.

Desmond: What do you get if you cross an
 elephant and a canary?
Dempsey: You tell me.
Desmond: A very messy cage.

Desmond: What officer takes care of the Army's
 finances?
Dempsey: I have no clue.
Desmond: The business major.

★ ★ ★

Desmond: What did one flag say to the other flag?
Dempsey: I can't guess.
Desmond: Nothing. It just waved!

My, My, My

My psychiatrist found out I have two personalities, so he charged me twice as much. I paid half and said, "Get the rest from the other guy."

My doctor is very conservative. If he doesn't need the money, he doesn't operate.

My brother's wife went to cooking school and learned how to prepare food in ten greasy lessons.

A man walks into a restaurant, orders a cup of coffee, and when it arrives, pours the coffee into an ashtray and eats the cup and saucer, leaving only the handle on the table. He then calls the waiter over and orders more coffee. As each cup arrives, he pours out the coffee and eats the cup and saucer. Pretty soon, there's nothing but a pile of china cup handles in front of him. He turns to the waiter and says, "You think I'm crazy, don't you?"

The waiter replies, "Yes, sir. The handle is the best part!"

My mom's cooking is so bad, we have holes in our screen door where the flies go out.

My doctor told me this operation was absolutely necessary. I said, "For what?" He said, "To send my kids to college."

My teenager daughter thinks freedom of speech gives her the right to make as many long-distance phone calls as she wants.

My gym teacher said I could be a real muscle man if I wanted to be. He says I have the head for it.

My uncle died and left me 200 clocks. I've been busy ever since winding up the estate.

My grandfather always used to ask me, "What's more important, your money or your health?" I'd say, "My health." He'd say, "Great, can you lend me 20 bucks?"

My Uncle Newt is as strong as a horse. We just wish he had the IQ of one.

My doctor insulted my looks last week. He told me I had a weak heart and advised me to avoid severe shocks. His prescription was to break every mirror in my house.

My neck's as stiff as a pipe, my head's like a lump of lead, and my nose is all stopped up. I don't need a doctor, I need a plumber.

I suffered for months with this ringing in my ear...until I got an unlisted ear.

"My father is certainly going to be surprised when I write to him," said the new graduate. "He always said I was so stupid that I couldn't even get a job. And in the last month I've had six!"

"My teacher sure does like me," a little boy said one day when he came home from school. "I heard her tell another teacher that it was the happiest day of her life when I was promoted to the third grade."

Our house is such a mess that the neighbors started a petition against us. Now we all have to wipe our feet before going out.

My wife's sister is so skinny that when she wears a fur coat she looks like a pipe cleaner.

My barber said, "Why don't you try something different for a change?" I said, "Okay, this time give me a good haircut."

11

Open the Door!

Knock, knock.
Who's there?
Patty.
Patty who?
Patty Cake, patty cake...

★ ★ ★

Knock, knock.
Who's there?
Arfur.
Arfur who?
Arfur Got.

★ ★ ★

Knock, knock.
Who's there?
Alex.
Alex who?
Alex plain later if you let me in.

★ ★ ★

Knock, knock.
Who's there?
Noah.
Noah who?
Noah good place to eat?

★ ★ ★

Knock, knock.
Who's there?
Bella.
Bella who?
Bella not working, that's why I knocka.

★ ★ ★

Knock, knock.
Who's there?
Sanctuary.
Sanctuary who?
Sanctuary much for answering the door.

★ ★ ★

Knock, knock.
Who's there?
Armageddon.
Armageddon who?
Armageddon out of here!

★ ★ ★

Knock, knock.
Who's there?

Oscar.
Oscar who?
Oscar silly question, get a silly answer.

★ ★ ★

Knock, knock.
Who's there?
Abby.
Abby who?
Abby birthday to you!

★ ★ ★

Knock, knock.
Who's there?
Hatch.
Hatch who?
Bless you.

★ ★ ★

Knock, knock.
Who's there?
Radio.
Radio who?
Radio not, here I come!

★ ★ ★

Knock, knock.
Who's there?
Arnie.
Arnie who?
Arnie going to let me in?

★ ★ ★

Knock, knock.
Who's there?
Jay.
Jay who?
Jay what you mean.

★ ★ ★

Knock, knock.
Who's there?
Howie.
Howie who?
Fine thanks. How are you?

★ ★ ★

Knock, knock.
Who's there?
Caesar.
Caesar who?
Caesar jolly good fellow.

Ebenezer and Egbert

Ebenezer: What wears shoes but doesn't have feet?
Egbert: Search me.
Ebenezer: A sidewalk.

★ ★ ★

Ebenezer: What is a computer's first sign of old age?
Egbert: I'm in the dark.
Ebenezer: Loss of memory.

★ ★ ★

Ebenezer: What do you get if you cross a parrot with a centipede?
Egbert: I'm blank.
Ebenezer: A great walkie-talkie.

★ ★ ★

Ebenezer: What kind of CDs do fish listen to?
Egbert: That's a mystery.
Ebenezer: Sole music.

Ebenezer: What do you call a lady way off in the distance?
Egbert: I have no idea.
Ebenezer: Dot.

Ebenezer: What is the difference between a sewing machine and a kiss on the lips?
Egbert: I don't know.
Ebenezer: One sews seams nice, the other seems so nice.

Ebenezer: What do you call a laughing hippo?
Egbert: I pass.
Ebenezer: A happypotamus.

Ebenezer: What do you get if you cross a parrot with a shark?
Egbert: Beats me.
Ebenezer: A bird that will talk your ear off.

Ebenezer: What kind of flowers do you give an absentminded squirrel?
Egbert: My mind is a blank.
Ebenezer: Forget-me-nuts.

★ ★ ★

Ebenezer: What do you call a mouse that can pick up an elephant?
Egbert: Who knows?
Ebenezer: Sir.

Ebenezer: What do you call a man with a car on his head?
Egbert: I give up.
Ebenezer: Jack.

Ebenezer: What's the easiest way to count a herd of cattle?
Egbert: You tell me.
Ebenezer: Use a cowculator.

Ebenezer: What car is parked in the tower of a famous Paris cathedral?
Egbert: I have no clue.
Ebenezer: The Hatchback of Notre Dame.

You Don't Say!

How did the Vikings communicate with one
   another?
By Norse code.

★ ★ ★

How do you fix a tomato?
With tomato paste.

★ ★ ★

How do pigs say goodbye?
With hogs and kisses.

★ ★ ★

How many bureaucrats does it take to screw in a
   light bulb?
*Two. One to assure everyone that everything possible is
   being done while the other screws the bulb into the
   water faucet.*

How many country musicians does it take to screw in a light bulb?
Five. One to do it, and four to sing about how much they're going to miss the old one.

How do you keep a monkey in suspense?
Give it a mirror and tell it to wait for the other monkey to say hi.

What do reindeer say before they tell a joke?
This one will sleigh you!

How do you make a car smile?
Take it on a joy ride.

★ ★ ★

How do you like my new jogging outfit?
I'm not sure. Run it by me again.

Laugh Out Loud

Suzy: They're a perfect match.
Steve: How do you know?
Suzy: He's a podiatrist...and she's always putting her foot in her mouth.

John: That's funny!
Cyndi: What is?
John: Oh, I was just thinking.
Cyndi: You're right, that is funny!

Robin: After we're married, would you live with me in the big forest near Nottingham?
Marian: Sherwood!

Nancy: I just saw an ocean liner that was stuck tight between two wooden docks.
Brian: Wow! Talk about pier pressure.

Tim: I sent away for some baby chickens to be delivered by mail, and they're not here yet.
Kristen: Relax. Your chicks are in the mail.

Christy: I'm going to sell light bulbs for a living.
Jon-Mark: Now that's a bright idea!

Jason: When does an Irish potato change its nationality?
Jacob: When it's made into a french fry.

Laura: When's your birthday?
Glenn: June nineteenth.
Laura: What year?
Glenn: Every year!

Kathy: When is the best time to take a Rottweiler for a walk?
Chris: Anytime he wants to go.

Sheryl: When's the best time to trim a beard?
Mike: Daylight shaving time.

Davy: My mother won't let dad do the cooking
   any more.
Anna: Why not?
Davy: Last night he burned the salad.

Bob: Have you heard the joke about the peacock?
Renee: No.
Bob: It's a beautiful tail.

Lora Lee: To whom do fish go to borrow money?
Paul: The loan shark.

Susan: Have you ever seen a man-eating tiger?
Mark: No, but in the cafe next door I once saw a
   man eating chicken!

Why, Why, Why?

Why did the banana go out with the prune?
Because he couldn't find a date.

Why was the little Egyptian boy confused?
Because his daddy was a mummy.

Why did the biscuit cry?
Because his mother had been a wafer so long.

Why was the robin first in line at the beauty
  parlor?
Because the early bird gets the perm.

Why was the Easter Bunny so upset?
He was having a bad hare day!

Why don't morons call 911 in an emergency?
They can't find the "eleven" button on the phone.

Why did you take my ornithology class?
Just for a lark.

Why are all these dry cleaning store owners
  gathered here?
They're holding a press conference.

Why did the police arrest the crow?
He was caught making crank caws.

Why is King Arthur wearing a cowboy hat and
  boots?
He's going to a squire dance.

Why is that skyscraper sneezing?
Maybe it has a building code.

Why did Ryan hit his birthday cake with a
  hammer?
Because Tyler said it was pound cake.

The Answer Man

Why do Irish peasants wear capes?
To cape them warm.

Why does a policeman have brass buttons on his coat?
To button it up.

Why was the baseball player arrested in the middle of the game?
He was caught stealing second base.

Why did the elephant wear green sneakers?
His blue ones were at the laundry.

Why does your sense of touch suffer when you
   are ill?
Because you don't feel well.

Why is a cat like a transcontinental highway?
Because it's fur from one end to the other.

Why wouldn't mother let the doctor operate on
   father?
Because she didn't want anybody else to open her male.

Why does it take longer to run from second base to
   third base than it takes to run from first base to
   second base?
Because there's a shortstop between second and third.

Why shouldn't you tell jokes when you're ice-
   skating?
Because the ice might crack up.

Why is it so hard to make frogs cry?
They're always hoppy.

Why do women not become bald as soon as men?
Because they wear their hair longer.

Why do people laugh up their sleeves?
Because that is where their funny bones are.

Why are dudes no longer imported into this
country from England?
Because a Yankee-doodle-doo.

Why did the silly kid put an alarm clock in his
shoe?
Because he didn't want his foot to fall asleep.

Why did the orange stop in the middle of the
road?
Because it ran out of juice.

Why do lions eat raw meat?
Because they don't know how to cook.

Why was the moron able to buy ice at half price?
Because it was melted.

Why would a compliment from a chicken be an
    insult?
Because it would be fowl language.

Why is the sea measured in knots?
They keep the ocean tied.

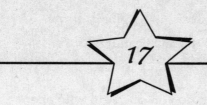

Ferdinand and Fargo

Ferdinand: What's the best thing to send to a couple who bought a house that has no water?
Fargo: Search me.
Ferdinand: A get well soon card.

Ferdinand: What brand of mouthwash do grouchy people use?
Fargo: I'm in the dark.
Ferdinand: Lister-mean.

Ferdinand: What's the difference between a crook and a bucket of dirt?
Fargo: I don't have the foggiest.
Ferdinand: The bucket.

Ferdinand: What do you do if your elephant
   squeaks?
Fargo: I'm blank.
Ferdinand: Give it some peanut oil.

Ferdinand: What do you call a girl with one
   trouser leg?
Fargo: I have no idea.
Ferdinand: Jean.

Ferdinand: What's black-and-white and comes out
   of the oven spitting mad?
Fargo: I don't know.
Ferdinand: A hot cross nun.

Ferdinand: What's purple and thousands of miles
   long?
Fargo: Beats me.
Ferdinand: The grape wall of China.

Ferdinand: What do you call the story of the Three
   Little Pigs?
Fargo: My mind is a blank.
Ferdinand: A pigtail.

Ferdinand: What is the cat's favorite TV show?
Fargo: Who knows?
Ferdinand: The Evening Mews.

Ferdinand: What has four legs and flies?
Fargo: I give up.
Ferdinand: A pig.

Ferdinand: What's brown and hops around in
    circles?
Fargo: You tell me.
Ferdinand: A kangaroo in a revolving door.

Ferdinand: What did the baby chick say when he
    saw his mother sitting on an orange?
Fargo: I can't guess.
Ferdinand: "Dad, dad, look what mama laid!"

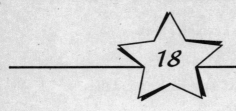

Gilbert and Gertrude

Gilbert: What's the best way to avoid being
   troubled by biting insects?
Gertrude: Search me.
Gilbert: Don't bite any!

Gilbert: What did the judge say when the skunk
   came into the courtroom?
Gertrude: I'm in the dark.
Gilbert: Odor in the court!

Gilbert: What do you call a reindeer with one eye?
Gertrude: I don't have the foggiest.
Gilbert: No idea.

Gilbert: What do you call 1,000 rats?
Gertrude: I'm blank.
Gilbert: Scary.

Gilbert: What did the buffalo say when his son left
for school each morning?
Gertrude: I have no idea.
Gilbert: Bison.

Gilbert: What famous author wrote about fruit?
Gertrude: I don't know.
Gilbert: William Shakespear.

Gilbert: What kind of girl does a hamburger like?
Gertrude: I pass.
Gilbert: Any girl named Patty!

Gilbert: What's gray, weighs two tons, and puts
you to sleep?
Gertrude: Beats me.
Gilbert: A hypnopotamus.

Gilbert: What can you see from the top of the Eiffel
Tower?
Gertrude: My mind is a blank.
Gilbert: Quite an eyeful!

★ ★ ★

Gilbert: What do frogs wear in the summer?
Gertrude: Who knows?
Gilbert: Open toad sandals.

★ ★ ★

Gilbert: What crime is committed at Thanksgiving
dinner?
Gertrude: I give up.
Gilbert: Pie-jacking!

★ ★ ★

Gilbert: What would you get if you crossed a
gorilla with the sixteenth U.S. president?
Gertrude: You tell me.
Gilbert: Ape Lincoln!

★ ★ ★

Gilbert: How do you like my poetry?
Gertrude: It could be worse!
Gilbert: That's a heck of a thing to say!
Gertrude: Okay, okay—it couldn't be worse!

Knee-Slappers

Mark: Someday I want to be cloned.
Deanna: Why make another fool of yourself?

Mike: My uncle spent a fortune on deodorants.
Susie: Was that before or after he found out that people didn't like him anyway?

Paul and Amy took their lunches to the local cafe to eat.

"Hey!" shouted the proprietor. "You can't eat your own food in here!"

"Okay," said Paul. So he and Amy swapped their sandwiches.

Carol: My boyfriend is so crazy.
Nancy: How crazy?
Carol: When the TV set was broken he went in the
other room and watched the radio.

Donna: Go look in the cage over there. You'll see a
ten-foot snake.
Larry: Don't try to kid me. I know snakes don't
have feet.

Becky: The town I live in is so small.
Frank: Really, how small?
Becky: Well, the road map is the actual size!

David: My birthday's coming. Do you know what
I need?
Charisse: Yeah, but how do you wrap a life?

Debbie: Our zoo is so messed up.
Brent: How messed up?
Debbie: So messed up that they crossed a cuddly
bear with a hobo and got a panda-handler.

Pete: Ouch! I have a splinter in my finger.
Ali: Scratching your head again?

Meg: Was that you singing as I came in?
Todd: Yes. I was killing time before my singing
  lesson.
Meg: Well, you were sure using the right weapon.

First goldfish: So I guess you're not dating that
  terrific-looking lobster anymore.
Second goldfish: It didn't work out. He was too
  shellfish.

Jan: Is it hard to bury a dead elephant?
Bud: Yes, it's a huge undertaking.

Pam: If I buy that TV, do I get a free clicker with it?
Bob: That's a remote possibility.

Melba: I used to run a doughnut shop.
Kenny: What happened?
Melba: I got tired of the hole business.

★ ★ ★

Melodi: My brother is so crazy.
Sher: How crazy?
Melodi: He saves burned-out light bulbs to use in
  his darkroom.

Huh?

Knock, knock.
Who's there?
Sam.
Sam who?
Sam day you'll recognize my voice.

★ ★ ★

Knock, knock.
Who's there?
Freeze.
Freeze who?
Freeze a jolly good fellow.

★ ★ ★

Knock, knock.
Who's there?
Sheila.
Sheila who?

Sheila be coming around the mountain when
   she comes.

Knock, knock.
Who's there?
Stu.
Stu who?
Stu late—I'm not going to tell you.

Knock, knock.
Who's there?
Venice.
Venice who?
Venice the next plane to Italy?

Knock, knock.
Who's there?
Germaine.
Germaine who?
Germaine you don't recognize me?

Knock, knock.
Who's there?
Thea.
Thea who?
Thea later, alligator.

Knock, knock.
Who's there?
Annabel.
Annabel who?
Annabel would be useful on this door.

Knock, knock.
Who's there?
Olga.
Olga who?
Olga home now.

Knock, knock.
Who's there?
Toby.
Toby who?
Toby or not to be.

Knock, knock.
Who's there?
Aida.
Aida who?
Aida whole box of chocolates, and I feel really sick.

Knock, knock.
Who's there?
Ben and Anna.

Ben and Anna who?
Ben and Anna split.

★ ★ ★

Knock, knock.
Who's there?
Marian.
Marian who?
Marian her little lamb.

★ ★ ★

Knock, knock.
Who's there?
Jess.
Jess who?
Don't know, you tell me.

★ ★ ★

Knock, knock.
Who's there?
Major.
Major who?
Major answer the door, didn't I?

Hanabel and Hector

Hanabel: What did the board say to the electric drill?
Hector: I'm in the dark.
Hanabel: You bore me.

★ ★ ★

Hanabel: What is green and pecks on trees?
Hector: I don't have the foggiest.
Hanabel: Woody Wood Pickle.

★ ★ ★

Hanabel: What happened to the baby chicken that misbehaved at school?
Hector: I'm blank.
Hanabel: It was eggspelled.

★ ★ ★

Hanabel: What game do mice like to play?
Hector: That's a mystery.
Hanabel: Hide and squeak.

Hanabel: What is the opposite of cock-a-doodle-doo?
Hector: I have no idea.
Hanabel: Cock-a-doodle-don't.

Hanabel: What do you call a woman who sets fire to her phone bill?
Hector: I don't know.
Hanabel: Bernadette.

Hanabel: What kind of schoolboy can jump higher than a house?
Hector: I pass.
Hanabel: All kinds—houses can't jump!

Hanabel: What do you call a bull who tells jokes?
Hector: Beats me.
Hanabel: Laugh-a-bull.

Hanabel: What kind of rabbits are good at fixing flat tires?

Hector: My mind is a blank.
Hanabel: Jackrabbits.

Hanabel: What do you call a deer with one eye and
no legs?
Hector: Who knows?
Hanabel: Still no idea.

Hanabel: What should you do if you swallow a
spoon?
Hector: I give up.
Hanabel: Lie down and don't stir.

Hanabel: What was the craziest battle of the
Revolutionary War?
Hector: You tell me.
Hanabel: The Battle of Bonkers Hill.

Hanabel: What's red, white, blue, and yellow?
Hector: I have no clue.
Hanabel: The Star-Spangled Banana!

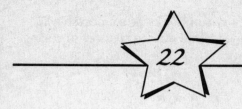

Doctor, Doctor!

Patient: Doctor, doctor! What's the best cure for flat feet?
Doctor: A foot pump.

★ ★ ★

Patient: Doctor, doctor! Every night my foot falls asleep.
Doctor: What's wrong with that?
Patient: It snores.

★ ★ ★

Patient: Doctor, help me. My wacky teenage son thinks he's a refrigerator.
Doctor: Stay calm. I'm sure he'll chill out.

★ ★ ★

Mother: Doctor, you've got to help my son. He thinks he's a smoke detector.
Doctor: Calm down. There's no cause for alarm.

80

Mother: Doctor, my son thinks he's a portable TV channel changer. What are the chances of curing him?
Doctor: Remote.

Patient: My doctor told me I was iron-deficient.
Friend: So what did you do?
Patient: I took up nail biting.

Doctor: I have a plan to make hair grow on bald men by feeding them natural cereal.
Scientist: Oh, no! Another hair-bran scheme.

Doctor: How bad is your insomnia?
Patient: It's bad. I haven't slept on the job in weeks.

Patient: Help me, Doc, I've got a fish stuck in my ear.
Doctor: I'm referring you to a specialist. You've got a serious herring problem.

★ ★ ★

Patient: Doctor, I have an eggplant growing out of my ear.

Doctor: Yes, I see it. That must be very irritating.
Patient: Sure is, Doc. I planted radishes!

★ ★ ★

Psychiatrist: You'll never make any progress until
   you get over these phobias.
Patient: I was afraid you'd say that.

★ ★ ★

Patient: I'm a failure!
Psychologist: Now, then, why don't you try the
   power of positive thinking?
Patient: All right. I'm positive I'm a failure!

★ ★ ★

Patient: I ate clams for the first time in my life yesterday and now I'm sick.
Doctor: Maybe they were bad. How did the clams
   look when you opened the shells?
Patient: Opened them?

★ ★ ★

Patient: Doctor, I have a terrible pain in my ear.
Doctor: Well, no wonder. There's a big bouquet of
   flowers in there. Where did it come from?
Patient: I haven't the faintest idea. Why don't you
   read the card?

★ ★ ★

Owner: Doctor! Doctor! I think my pet vulture's
   dying of flu.

Doctor: Vultures don't die of flu.
Owen: This one will. It flew under a bus.

School doctor: Have you ever had trouble with
   appendicitis?
Owen: Only when I tried to spell it.

Silly Dillies

Jennifer: They say you should wash your hands after handling money, because the bills are covered with germs.

Julie: I'm not in any danger—even a germ couldn't live on the money I make!

Jewelry shop owner: How's business this morning?

Salesman: You won't believe this, sir, but I've sold five diamond tiaras already this morning!

Jewelry shop owner: Looks like a real tiara boom today!

Jacob: Are you buying Christmas seals this year?

Nate: Certainly not. What would I feed them?

Mike: I'm going on a strict diet.
Joy: Like the last one—no eating between snacks?

Jeff: Two slices of bread are getting married.
Matt: Well, let's toast the happy couple.

Private: Hey, Sarge! Where do baby soldiers get their basic training?
Sarge: At bootie camp.

Jan: Do you like my new outfit?
Jon: Honey, it's in a clash by itself.

Barry: Do psychologists have their own union?
Stacey: Of course, silly: The United Mind Workers.

Lisa: Yuck! Your breath smells like garbage.
Ryan: It's not my fault! I had junk food for lunch.

Two bums were walking along in a park.

One said suddenly, "Awww, look at the dead birdie."

The other stopped, looked up, and asked, "Where?"

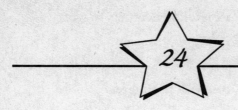

Daffy Dictionary

Actor: A person who works really hard at never being himself.

★ ★ ★

Bee: A real buzz word.

★ ★ ★

Bacteria: Rear entrance to a cafeteria.

★ ★ ★

A baby chicken coop: Cheep housing.

★ ★ ★

Claustrophobia: Fear of Santa.

★ ★ ★

Diet plan: Fast thinking.

Psychiatrist: A person who never has to worry as long as others do.

Fireflies: Mosquitoes with flashlights.

Fitness trainer: A person who lives off the fat of the land.

Flashlight: A plastic or metal container for dead batteries.

Hurricane: What Abel said to his brother when he was late for school.

Kleptomania: The gift of grab.

Lamp designer: A person who is lightheaded.

Miser: A commander-in-cheap.

Misfortune: Daughter of Mr. and Mrs. Fortune.

Operetta: An employee of the phone company.

Paradox: A couple of physicians.

Prison: The place you'd go only in a pinch.

Ring announcer: A minister at a wedding.

Roof repair person: A person who likes to stay on top of things at work.

Seamstress: A real material girl.

Skeleton: Bones with the people off.

Inflation: That's when something you bought for $5 last year costs $10 to repair.

Sleeping bag: A nap sack.

Conscience: That still small voice that tells you your parents might check up on you.

Steering committee: Two backseat drivers.

Ventriloquist: A person who enjoys talking to himself.

Wind: Air that's late for work.

An insulting telegram: A barbed wire.

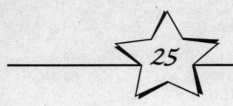

Ivan and Isadora

Ivan: What did the Eskimo schoolboy say to the Eskimo schoolgirl?
Isadora: Search me.
Ivan: What's an ice girl like you doing in a place like this?

Ivan: What do you call a golfer with an IQ of 125?
Isadora: I'm in the dark.
Ivan: A foursome.

Ivan: What do you get if you cross a cocker spaniel, a poodle, and a rooster?
Isadora: I don't have the foggiest.
Ivan: A cockapoodledoo!

Ivan: What do you call a lazy butcher?
Isadora: I'm blank.
Ivan: A meatloafer.

Ivan: What is the best thing to take into the desert?
Isadora: That's a mystery.
Ivan: A thirst-aid kit.

Ivan: What do skunks read?
Isadora: I have no idea.
Ivan: Best-smellers.

Ivan: What's black and white and makes a lot of
    noise?
Isadora: I don't know.
Ivan: A zebra with a set of drums.

Ivan: What do you call two identically masked
    men?
Isadora: I pass.
Ivan: The Clone Rangers.

Ivan: What does the music teacher do when he's
    locked out of the classroom?
Isadora: Beats me.
Ivan: Sings until he gets the right key.

Ivan: What kind of music do chemists listen to?
Isadora: My mind is a blank.
Ivan: Acid rock.

Ivan: What do you get if you cross a crocodile with
a rose?
Isadora: Who knows?
Ivan: I don't know, either. But I wouldn't try
smelling it.

Ivan: What did the Indian call the pilgrim with a
bucket over his head?
Isadora: You tell me.
Ivan: Pailface.

Ivan: What kind of tree is often found in the
kitchen?
Isadora: I have no clue.
Ivan: A pantry!

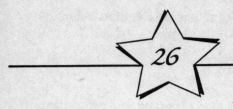

Odds and Ends

Plumber: I can't finish putting in your bathroom fixtures until next month.

Homeowner: Now that's a shower stall if I ever heard one.

Financier: Young man, you've asked me for a dollar every morning for the last six months. Why don't you just hit me up for a hundred dollars and get it over with?

Panhandler: It seems imprudent to put all one's begs in one ask it.

"It's no use. Art doesn't listen to me," said a little boy who was praying for a bike.

"Art who?" asked the boy's mother.

"Art in heaven," came the reply.

★ ★ ★

"Why are you scratching your head?"
"I've got those arithmetic bugs again."
"Arithmetic bugs—what are they?"
"Well, some people call them head lice."
"Then why do you call them arithmetic bugs?"
"Because they add to my misery, subtract from my
   pleasure, divide my attention, and multiply like
   crazy."

★ ★ ★

"Why are you crying, Jim?" asked the teacher.
"Because my parrot died last night. I washed it
   with Tide soap."
"Jim," said the teacher, "didn't you know that Tide
   is bad for parrots?"
"Oh, it wasn't the Tide that killed it. It was the spin
   cycle."

★ ★ ★

A man was trying to return a cat to the pet shop.
"You said this cat would be good for mice. I've had
   him for three weeks and nothing! Not a single
   mouse."
"Well," said the shopkeeper, "that's good for mice,
   isn't it?"

Customer: Have you got any dogs going cheap?
Pet shop owner: No, I'm afraid all our dogs go
   "woof."

★ ★ ★

Harry: The wedding's off!

Larry: I thought you two were crazy about each other?!

Harry: So did I, until she told me she'd be true to the end.

Larry: Sounds good to me...

Harry: But I'm a quarterback!

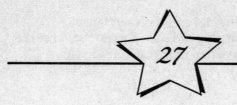

Why Not?

Why is twice ten the same as twice eleven?
Because twice ten is twenty, and twice eleven is twenty, too.

Why does Santa always climb down chimneys?
Because it soots him.

Is it dangerous to swim on a full stomach?
Well, it's better to swim in water!

Why did the ram fall over the cliff?
He didn't see the ewe turn.

What is the best way to communicate with a fish?
Drop it a line.

Why are dolphins cleverer than humans?
*Within three hours they can train a man to stand at the
side of a pool and feed them fish.*

Why did the sea bird rob the jewelry store?
Because diamonds are a gull's best friend.

Why did Ken keep his trumpet in the fridge?
Because he liked cool music.

Why did the golfer wear an extra pair of trousers?
In case he got a hole in one.

Why did the antelope run?
Nobody gnu.

Why did the crazy man eat a light bulb?
Because he was in need of light refreshment.

Why did the dog go to court?
To pay a barking ticket.

School's Out

Teacher: Have you ever seen a windowbox?
Joshua: No, but I've seen a garden fence.

Mr. Anderson: What's your son going to be when he's passed all his exams and left school?
Mr. Wapnick: At the rate he's going, a senior citizen.

Teacher: You missed school yesterday, didn't you?
Pupil: No, sir, I didn't miss it at all.

Little boy: When I grow up I want to make millions and live in a mansion that has no bathtubs.
Teacher: Why do you want to live in a mansion with no bathtubs?
Little boy: I want to be filthy rich!

Algebra teacher: And in conclusion, class, we finally learn that X is equal to zero.
Student: Humph! All that work for nothing.

Alissa: My teacher talks to himself. Does yours?
Jared: Yes. But she thinks we're listening to her.

Taylor: I wish I'd been born hundreds of years ago.
Amanda: Why's that?
Taylor: I wouldn't have had so much history to learn.

Hopeless Noel: I've thought of a way of making the school football team more successful.
Jack: Oh, are you leaving it?

Jill: Does your school play have a happy ending?
Bud: I'll say! I was very happy when it had ended.

What problem did the cross-eyed teacher have?
She couldn't control her pupils.

★ ★ ★

Teacher: Can you spell your name backwards, Simon?

Simon: No, mis.

Teacher: Sally, one of your essays is very good but the other one I can't read.

Sally: Yes, sir. My mother is a much better writer than my father.

Teacher: Can you name something that's harder than a diamond?

Student: Yes—paying for one.

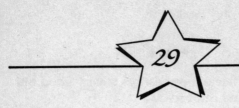

Jonah and Jordan

Jonah: What do whales like to chew?
Jordan: Search me.
Jonah: Blubber gum.

★ ★ ★

Jonah: What is Santa's favorite cowboy song?
Jordan: I'm in the dark.
Jonah: Ho-Ho-Home on the Range.

★ ★ ★

Jonah: What do you call a snake who gets elected mayor?
Jordan: I don't have the foggiest.
Jonah: A civil serpent.

★ ★ ★

Jonah: What do you get when you cross a chicken with a bell?

Jordan: I'm blank.
Jonah: You get an alarm cluck.

Jonah: What lives under the sea and carries a lot of
     people?
Jordan: That's a mystery.
Jonah: An octobus.

Jonah: What do you call a man who steals a lot?
Jordan: I don't know.
Jonah: Robin.

Jonah: What would you get if you crossed a pig
     with a rooster?
Jordan: I pass.
Jonah: An animal that goes "Oink-a-doodle-doo!"

Jonah: What gives milk, says "moo, moo" and
     makes all your dreams come true?
Jordan: Beats me.
Jonah: Your dairy godmother.

★ ★ ★

Jonah: What state is always happy?
Jordan: My mind is a blank.
Jonah: Merryland.

Jonah: What do you call a girl with a frog on her
head?
Jordan: Who knows?
Jonah: Lily.

Jonah: What do you get from an Alaskan cow?
Jordan: I give up.
Jonah: Cold cream.

Jonah: What's the best way to stuff a turkey?
Jordan: You tell me.
Jonah: Take him out for pizza and ice cream!

★ ★ ★

Jonah: What's the difference between one of
Columbus' sailors and a class clown?
Jordan: I have no clue.
Jonah: One left his Spain behind and the other left
his brain behind.

Come In

Knock, knock.
Who's there?
Puffin.
Puffin who?
Puffin' and pantin'—ran all the way here.

★ ★ ★

Knock, knock.
Who's there?
Canoe.
Canoe who?
Canoe hurry up and let me in?

★ ★ ★

Knock, knock.
Who's there?
Albert.
Albert who?
Albert you'll never guess.

★ ★ ★

Knock, knock.
Who's there?
Juicy.
Juicy who?
Juicy what I see?

★ ★ ★

Knock, knock.
Who's there?
Althea.
Althea who?
Althea later, alligator.

★ ★ ★

Knock, knock.
Who's there?
Lettuce.
Lettuce who?
Lettuce in and we'll tell you.

★ ★ ★

Knock, knock.
Who's there?
Iris.
Iris who?
Iris you would open the door.

★ ★ ★

Knock, knock.
Who's there?

Dots.
Dots who?
Dots for me to know, and you to find out.

Knock, knock.
Who's there?
Hawaii.
Hawaii who?
I'm fine, Hawaii you?

Knock, knock.
Who's there?
Cole.
Cole who?
Cole as a cucumber.

Knock, knock.
Who's there?
Ann.
Ann who?
Ann amazingly good knock-knock joke.

Knock, knock.
Who's there?
Nana.
Nana who?
Nana your business.

★ ★ ★

Knock, knock.
Who's there?
Emma.
Emma who?
Emma bit cold out here, will you let me in?

★ ★ ★

Knock, knock.
Who's there?
Midas.
Midas who?
Midas well let me in.

★ ★ ★

Knock, knock.
Who's there?
Harmony.
Harmony who?
Harmony times must I tell you not to do that!

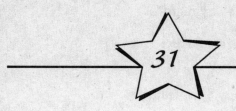

Have You Heard?

Jon: Did you hear about the new Broadway musical with the singing and dancing sardines?
Jen: Search me.
Jon: I hear the show is really packing them in.

Ted: Did you hear about the dentist who became a brain surgeon?
Jenny: I'm in the dark.
Ted: His drill slipped.

Jimmy: Did you hear about the schoolboy who just couldn't come to grips with decimals?
Kendra: Not yet.
Jimmy: He couldn't see the point.

★ ★ ★

Ricky: Did you hear about the monster who ate bits of metal every night?
Nova: I'm blank.
Ricky: It was his staple diet.

Don: Did you buy duck feathers?
Susan: No, why?
Don: Well, they were marked down.

Eric: Did you hear the joke about the ocean?
JB: Tell me.
Eric: Never mind. It's too deep for you.

Norm: Did you hear the joke about the rotten pudding?
Patsy: I have no idea.
Norm: Never mind. You wouldn't swallow it.

Tom: Did you hear the joke about the hole in the ground?
Kim: I don't know.
Tom: Never mind. You wouldn't dig it.

Bryan: What do you think about intuition?
Yvonne: Not much. Do you?
Bryan: No, but I have a feeling I might someday.

★ ★ ★

Chris: Did you hear NASA's planning to put 500
  cows into orbit?
Christina: Wow!
Chris: Yeah, it'll be the herd shot around the world.

★ ★ ★

Johnnie: Did you hear the one about the farmer
  who turned his south forty into an auto parts
  junkyard?
Becky: I don't think so.
Johnnie: Every year was a bumper crop.

Karlotta and Katrina

Karlotta: Where do rabbits go when they get married?
Katrina: Search me.
Karlotta: On their bunnymoon.

★ ★ ★

Karlotta: Where did the flying elephant land?
Katrina: I'm in the dark.
Karlotta: At the earport.

★ ★ ★

Karlotta: Where do old car tires end up?
Katrina: I don't have the foggiest.
Karlotta: On skid row.

★ ★ ★

Karlotta: Where do you park a truckload of pigs?
Katrina: I'm blank.
Karlotta: In an empty porking place!

Karlotta: Where does a pickle love to eat?
Katrina: That's a mystery.
Karlotta: In a dilly catessen!

Karlotta: Where do geologists go for entertainment?
Katrina: I have no idea.
Karlotta: To rock concerts.

Karlotta: Where do birds invest their money?
Katrina: I don't know.
Karlotta: In the stork market.

Karlotta: Where does Batman keep his goldfish?
Katrina: I pass.
Karlotta: In the bat tub.

Karlotta: Where do shellfish go to borrow money?
Katrina: Beats me.
Karlotta: To the prawn-broker.

Karlotta: Where does seaweed look for a job?
Katrina: My mind is a blank.
Karlotta: In the kelp-wanted ads.

Karlotta: Where is the dead center of Boston?
Katrina: Who knows?
Karlotta: The cemetery.

Karlotta: Where do dogs wash their clothes?
Katrina: I give up.
Karlotta: At the laundromutt.

Karlotta: Where do burgers like to dance?
Katrina: You tell me.
Karlotta: At a meat ball!

Karlotta: Where do you buy cats from?
Katrina: I have no clue.
Karlotta: A catalogue.

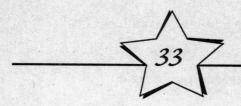

Giggles

Verna: My father has Washington's shoe.
Molly: That's nothing. My father has Adam's apple.

Terry: What do you do?
Shawna: I'm a dairy maid in a candy factory.
Terry: So what do you do?
Shawna: I milk chocolates.

Larry: I couldn't sleep last night.
Jerry: Why not?
Larry: I plugged the electric blanket into the toaster by mistake, and I kept popping out of bed all night.

Mack: Are you a Giant fan?
Jack: Yes.
Mack: Well, I'm a little air conditioner.

★ ★ ★

Barbie: I'm engaged to an Irishman.
Laurie: Oh, really?
Barbie: No, O'Reilly.

★ ★ ★

Melody: I was in hot water last night.
Marcy: Why is that?
Melody: I had to take a bath.

★ ★ ★

Mother: I hear you've been fighting with one of
those boys next door and have given him a
black eye.
Son: Yes, ma'am. You see, they're twins, and I
wanted some way to tell them apart.

★ ★ ★

Lady: Give me a ticket to Toledo.
Agent: Do you want to go by Buffalo?
Lady: No, I prefer to go by train.

★ ★ ★

Karl: Did you hear about the skunk who couldn't
swim?
Eli: No, what about him?
Karl: He stank to the bottom of the pool.

Private: I've come to see General Parker.
Sergeant: I'm sorry, but the general is sick today.
Private: What made him sick?
Sergeant: Oh, things in general.

Boy: You need to learn more about baseball. Do you know what RBI stands for?
Girl: Really Boring Information.

Nit: What do you call a 200-pound man with a club?
Wit: Sir!

Mother: Auntie will never kiss you with a dirty face.
Son: That's what I thought.

Bill: I wish I had enough money to buy an elephant.
Jill: What in the world do you want an elephant for?
Bill: I don't. I just wish I had that much money.

Mother: Son, the canary has disappeared.
Son: That's funny. It was there when I cleaned the cage with the vacuum cleaner.

First sardine: How do you hug a hungry shark?
Second sardine: Very carefully.

Lydia: Where did he meet her?
Lucile: They met in a revolving door, and he's been
    going around with her ever since.

★ ★ ★

Rex: I went to see my girl last night.
Tex: Did you stay late?
Rex: Well, I guess I did, but I kept turning the
    clock back. Finally my girl's father yelled down
    from upstairs and said: "That clock has struck
    12 three times now—would you mind letting it
    practice on one for a while?"

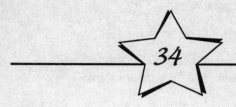

Tell Me Why!

Why is a tent like a baseball?
Because they both have to be pitched.

 ★ ★ ★

Why did the boy hold his report card over his head?
He was trying to raise his grades.

 ★ ★ ★

Why did you put a worm in your sister's bed?
I couldn't find an iguana.

 ★ ★ ★

Why did the woman spray insect repellent on her computer?
The program had a bug in it.

 ★ ★ ★

Why should men avoid the letter A?
Because it makes men mean.

Why did the crow sit on the telephone line?
Because he was making a long-distance caw.

Why is the letter K like a pig's tail?
Because it is at the end of pork.

Why are cards like wolves?
Because they belong to a pack.

Why did the football coach send in his second
string?
To tie up the game.

Why did the boy jump in the mud, and then cross
the street twice?
Because he was a dirty double-crosser.

Why did the dieter bring scissors to the dinner
table?
Because he wanted to cut calories.

Why are tomatoes the slowest fruit?
They're always trying to ketchup.

Why did the worm oversleep?
Because he didn't want to be caught by the early bird.

Why did the robber take a shower before holding up the bank?
He wanted to make sure he'd have a clean getaway.

Why are football players cool?
Because they have a lot of fans.

Why is a horse like a lollipop?
Because the more you lick it the faster it goes.

Why did the judge sentence the comedian to five years in jail?
He was involved in some funny business.

Why does a cow go over a hill?
Because she can't go under it.

Why does a man permit himself to be hen-pecked?
Because he's chicken-hearted.

Why was the owl a poor student?
He just didn't give a hoot!

Lila and Lorenzo

Lila: What would you call it if your wedding day
was December 25?
Lorenzo: Search me.
Lila: A Marry Christmas!

Lila: What would you get if you crossed a long-
legged insect with a donkey?
Lorenzo: I'm in the dark.
Lila: A braying mantis.

Lila: What do teenage ducks worry about?
Lorenzo: I don't have the foggiest.
Lila: Getting goose pimples.

Lila: What have you got that'll cure fleas on a
  dog?
Lorenzo: I'm blank.
Lila: Depends on what's ailing the fleas.

Lila: What wallows in mud and carries colored
  eggs?
Lorenzo: That's a mystery.
Lila: The Easter Piggy.

Lila: What fish only swims at night?
Lorenzo: I have no idea.
Lila: A starfish.

Lila: What do you call a monster with gravy, meat,
  and potatoes on his head?
Lorenzo: I don't know.
Lila: Stew.

Lila: What did one pickle say to the other?
Lorenzo: I pass.
Lila: You mean a great dill to me.

Lila: What do you call a person who makes minia-
  ture watches?

Lorenzo: Beats me.
Lila: A small-time operator.

Lila: What do you call a man with a beach on his
head?
Lorenzo: My mind is a blank.
Lila: Sandy.

Lila: What do you call a dead elephant?
Lorenzo: Who knows?
Lila: Nothing. He can't hear you.

Lila: What did the farmer call the cow that
wouldn't give him any milk?
Lorenzo: I give up.
Lila: An udder failure.

Lila: What happened at the milking competition?
Lorenzo: You tell me.
Lila: Udder chaos.

★ ★ ★

Lila: What do you call the head of a corporation
who makes a lot of business blunders?
Lorenzo: I have no clue.
Lila: A CEO-oh.

★ ★ ★

Lila: What did the student fish bring to school for his teacher?
Lorenzo: I can't guess.
Lila: A crab apple.

How Now?

How do you prevent water from getting into your house?
Stop paying the water bill.

How did the gorilla break out of its cage?
With a monkey wrench.

How do they prevent crime at McDonald's?
With a burger alarm!

How do vegetables trace their ancestry?
They go back to their roots.

How do bunnies stay cool in the summertime?
They buy a good hare conditioner.

How do you make an elephant stew?
Keep it waiting at the doctor's office.

How does one angel greet another?
By saying, "Halo!"

How do you cure a headache?
Put your head through a window, and the pane will dis-appear.

How do you get rid of a boomerang?
Throw it down a one-way street.

How do you catch a school of fish?
With a bookworm.

How did the computer criminal get out of jail?
Pressed the escape key.

How do you stop an elephant from chasing you?
With elephant repellent.

How do you get six elephants in a matchbox?
Well, first you have to take the matches out.

How do you find your dog if he's lost in the
woods?
Just put your ear to a tree and listen for the bark.

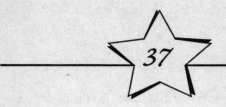

More Craziness

Eskimo boy: I drove a dogsled across the Arctic just to see you.
Eskimo girl: Oh, that's a lot of mush.

Tyler: You know, I used to go around with her until I found out she spent $5000 a year on dresses.
Owen: So you broke up over that?
Tyler: Yeah. Now I'm going with her dressmaker.

Freshman: I went out for the football team today, and I think I made it.
Junior: What makes you think you made the team?
Freshman: Well, the coach took one look at me and said, "Oh, no, this is the end!"

Football player: Coach, my doctor says I can't play
 football.
Coach: You didn't have to go to a doctor. I could
 have told you that.

Christina: I just can't find the man who'll make the
 perfect husband.
Sara: Maybe you're expecting too much?
Christina: Nonsense! All I'm looking for is a man
 who's kind and understanding. Is that too much
 to ask of a millionaire?

Motorist: How did you manage to eliminate the
 bad roads in this part of the country?
Farmer: Simple. When the going gets rugged, we
 don't call it a road; we call it a detour.

Tammy: He was wonderful. Divine. He said things
 to me no man ever said.
Annie: What was that?
Tammy: He asked me to marry him.

Mother: What are you doing, Anna Mae?
Anna Mae: I'm writing a letter to my friend, Cindy.
Mother: But you don't know how to write.
Anna Mae: That's okay! Cindy doesn't know how
 to read.

★ ★ ★

James (at the movies): Can you see all right?
Natalie: Yes.
James: Is there a draft on you?
Natalie: No.
James: Is your seat comfortable?
Natalie: Yes.
James: Will you change places with me?

First cowboy: He's a real tough hombre. Quick on
   the trigger, too. His guns are blazing before they
   clear the holster.
Second cowboy: What's his name?
First cowboy: No-Toes Smith.

Man: I'm in a hurry. Will the pancakes be long?
Waiter: No, sir, they will be round.

Willard: Excuse me, I think you are sitting in my
   seat.
Tough guy: Yeah? Prove it.
Willard: I left my pie and ice cream on it.

Barber: Well, my little man, and how would you
   like your hair cut?

Small boy: If you please, sir, just like my father's—
and don't forget the little round hole at the top
where the head comes through.

Girl: Would you love me just the same if my father
lost all his money?
Boy: He hasn't lost it, has he?
Girl: No.
Boy: Of course, I would, you silly girl.

Little boy (calling father at office): Hello, who is
this?
Father (recognizing his son's voice): The smartest
man in the world.
Little boy: Oh, I must have the wrong number.

Ella: Would you rather have an elephant chase you
or a lion?
Reginald: I would rather have the elephant chase
the lion.

Norris: Well, how are you getting on in your new
ten-room house?
Boris: Oh, not so badly. We furnished one of the
bedrooms by collecting soap coupons.
Norris: Didn't you furnish the other nine rooms?
Boris: We can't. They're full of soap.

Mama owl: I'm worried about Junior.
Papa owl: What's the matter?
Mama owl: He just doesn't give a hoot about anything.

Judge: Why did you hit your dentist?
Man: Because he got on my nerves.

★ ★ ★

Harry: My big brother shaves every day.
Larry: That's nothing! Mine shaves 50 times a day.
Harry: He must be crazy.
Larry: No, he's a barber.

★ ★ ★

Boy: Oh, darling, I love you so much. Please say you'll be mine. I'm not rich like Quinten Everrich. I haven't a car, or a fine house, or a well-stocked cellar like Quinten does. But darling, I love you. I cannot live without you.
Girl: And I love you, too, darling; but, where is this guy Quinten Everrich?

Stop that Knocking!

Knock, knock.
Who's there?
Celeste.
Celeste who?
Celeste time I come calling.

★ ★ ★

Knock, knock.
Who's there?
Earl.
Earl who?
Earl tell you if you open the door.

★ ★ ★

Knock, knock.
Who's there?
Police.
Police who?
Police open the door.

Knock, knock.
Who's there?
Xavier.
Xavier who?
Xavier breath! I'm not leaving.

Knock, knock.
Who's there?
Fido.
Fido who?
Fido known you were here, I'd have baked a cake.

Knock, knock.
Who's there?
Elly.
Elly who?
Elly Mentary, my dear Watson.

Knock, knock.
Who's there?
Wooden shoe.
Wooden shoe who?
Wooden shoe like to know?

Knock, knock.
Who's there?
Iran.
Iran who?
Iran all the way home.

★ ★ ★

Knock, knock.
Who's there?
Hank.
Hank who?
You're welcome.

★ ★ ★

Knock, knock.
Who's there?
Annie.
Annie who?
Annie body home?

★ ★ ★

Knock, knock.
Who's there?
José.
Jose' who?
Jose', can you see?

★ ★ ★

Knock, knock.
Who's there?
Jewel.

Jewel who?
Jewel know who when you open the door.

Knock, knock.
Who's there?
Irish.
Irish who?
Irish you a Merry Christmas!

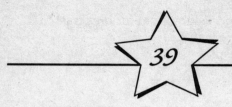

Malcolm and Matilda

Malcolm: What did Cinderella say when she took her photos to be developed?
Matilda: Search me.
Malcolm: Some day my prints will come.

Malcolm: What did the rake say to the hoe?
Matilda: I'm in the dark.
Malcolm: Hi, hoe!

Malcolm: What's the largest thing ever made of grapes?
Matilda: I don't have the foggiest.
Malcolm: The grape wall of China.

Malcolm: What do you say if you meet a toad?
Matilda: I'm blank.
Malcolm: Wart's new?

★ ★ ★

Malcolm: What do Eskimos eat for breakfast?
Matilda: That's a mystery.
Malcolm: Ice Krispies.

★ ★ ★

Malcolm: What do you call a man in a pile of
  leaves?
Matilda: I have no idea.
Malcolm: Russell.

★ ★ ★

Malcolm: What do you call a teacher with a cat on
  her head?
Matilda: I don't know.
Malcolm: Kitty.

★ ★ ★

Malcolm: What do you give a horse with a
  cold?
Matilda: I pass.
Malcolm: Cough stirrup.

★ ★ ★

Malcolm: What happened when the owl lost his
  voice?
Matilda: Beats me.
Malcolm: He didn't give a hoot.

★ ★ ★

Malcolm: What did Julius Caesar's doctor say when Julius Caesar came down with the sniffles?
Matilda: My mind is a blank.
Malcolm: Hail, Sneezer!

★ ★ ★

Malcolm: What is the favorite snack of computer programmers?
Matilda: Who knows?
Malcolm: Chips.

★ ★ ★

Malcolm: What did the preacher say at the pickle wedding?
Matilda: I give up.
Malcolm: Dilly beloved, we are gathered here together...!

★ ★ ★

Malcolm: What do you get when you cross a hog with a tree?
Matilda: You tell me.
Malcolm: Porky Twig.

★ ★ ★

Malcolm: What is made of wood but can't be sawed?
Matilda: I have no clue.
Malcolm: Sawdust.

★ ★ ★

Malcolm: What's an astronaut's favorite part of a computer?
Matilda: I can't guess.
Malcolm: The spacebar.

Laugh and Learn

Teacher: What happened when the wheel was invented?
Pupil: It caused a revolution.

Teacher: Your books are a disgrace, Ian. I don't see how anyone can possibly make as many mistakes in one day as you do.
Ian: I get here early, sir.

Teacher: I wish you'd pay a little attention!
Pupil: I'm paying as little as I can, sir.

Reader: Can you tell me where the self-help section is?
Librarian: Wouldn't that rather defeat the purpose?

Q: There were ten zebras in the zoo. All but nine escaped. How many were left?
A: Nine!

Teacher: What's your name?
Pupil: George.
Teacher: Say "sir" when you speak to me.
Pupil: All right, Sir George.

Teacher: Why are you late this time, son?
Student: I broke my ankle, sir.
Teacher: That's a lame excuse.

Teacher: When was the Iron Age?
Pupil: Before they invented drip-dry shirts?

Mr. Anderson: I hear your daughter became a writer when she left school. Does she write for money?
Mr. Postune: Yes, almost every letter we get.

English teacher: Now give me a sentence using the word "fascinate."

Student: My raincoat has ten buttons but I can only fasten eight.

One day a teacher came into her classroom and found a very rude word chalked on her blackboard.

"I'm not going to scold," she said. "We're going to take care of this by the honor system. We'll all close our eyes and I'll count up to 100. When we open our eyes whoever wrote that will have tip-toed up to the board and erased it."

Everyone closed their eyes.

"One...two...three..."

Pitter patter.

"...48...49...50..."

Squeak, squeak.

"...99...100."

Everyone opened their eyes and there, on the board, was another rude word and above it was chalked, "The phantom writer strikes again."

The young teacher was complaining to her friends about how badly she was being paid. "We get a really poultry amount each month," she said.

"You mean 'paltry,' " corrected one of her friends.

"No, I don't. I mean 'poultry,' " replied the teacher. "What I earn is chicken feed."

41

Nina and Nola

Nina: What did the snow guy say to the beautiful snow gal?
Nola: Search me.
Nina: Do you believe in love at frost sight?

Nina: What goes "oink-oink" and steals your money?
Nola: I'm in the dark.
Nina: A pig-pocket.

Nina: What did the rabbit say when he fell into a hole filled with water?
Nola: I don't have the foggiest.
Nina: Oh, well.

Nina: What are the three great American parties?
Nola: I'm blank.
Nina: Democratic, Republican, and Tupperware.

Nina: What do you call a gorilla with headphones on?
Nola: That's a mystery.
Nina: Anything you like. He can't hear you.

Nina: What bread is dangerous?
Nola: I have no idea.
Nina: Attila the Bun.

Nina: What did the farmer say when he found a hole in one of his pumpkins?
Nola: I don't know.
Nina: I think I need a pumpkin patch.

Nina: What's the hardest thing about learning to ride a horse?
Nola: I pass.
Nina: The ground!

Nina: What's bent, salty, and sings?
Nola: Beats me.
Nina: Elvis Pretzel.

Nina: What happened to the cat that swallowed a ball of wool?
Nola: My mind is a blank.
Nina: She had mittens.

★ ★ ★

Nina: What has 12 legs, 6 eyes, 3 tails, and can't see?
Nola: Who knows?
Nina: Three blind mice.

★ ★ ★

Nina: What would you be after a free lunch in a vineyard?
Nola: I give up.
Nina: Grapeful.

★ ★ ★

Nina: What state can tell the most jokes?
Nola: You tell me.
Nina: Jokelahoma.

★ ★ ★

Nina: What do you call a bunch of chickens playing hide-and-seek?
Nola: I have no clue.
Nina: Fowl play.

Leftovers

Golfer: You're such a lousy caddy! When we get back to the clubhouse I'm going to see that you get fired.
Caddy: It's okay with me. By the time we get back to the clubhouse I'll be old enough to get a regular job!

Customer: This lumber has holes in it!
Hardware clerk: Those are knotholes.
Customer: Look, buddy, if those are not holes, what are they?

Byron: Boy, do I feel lousy. I've been on a train for three hours, riding backwards the whole time.
Becki: Why didn't you switch seats with the person across from you?

Byron: I would've, but there was no one in the seat across from me.

Tourist: Excuse me, but do you have a pumpkin patch?
Farmer: Why, do you have a leaky pumpkin?

After hearing the story about how God took the rib out of Adam's side, a little boy who had been running and had gotten a side ache replied to his mother: "I think I'm going to have a wife."

Sonny: I finally got my brother to stop biting his nails.
Tim: How?
Sonny: I got him to put on his shoes.

Curtis: At my piano teacher's last performance the audience cheered and cheered.
Sam: Why?
Curtis: Because the piano was locked!

Grandfather clock: It's now 3:00.
Alarm clock: You're wrong. It's 3:30.
Grandfather clock: Don't tock back to me, young fella.

Show me a good loser...and I'll show you a fellow playing tennis with his teacher.

Customer: What's the secret recipe for your delicious homemade bread?
Baker: Sorry. The recipe is classified on a knead the dough basis.

★ ★ ★

Boss: Our new billing clerk needs to see a psychiatrist.
Secretary: Why?
Boss: She keeps hearing strange invoices.

Bible Talk

Teacher: Do you know who built the Ark?
Student: No.
Teacher: Correct.

★ ★ ★

What is the sharpest tool mentioned in the Bible?
The Acts of the Apostles.

★ ★ ★

Why was Job always cold in bed?
Because he had such miserable comforters.

★ ★ ★

Wife: Would you help me with the dishes?
Husband: That isn't a man's job.
Wife: The Bible suggests that it is.
Husband: Where does it say that?

Wife: In 2 Kings 21:13 it says, "And I will wipe
Jerusalem as a man wipeth a dish, wiping it and
turning it upside down."

Who was the strongest man in the Bible?
Jonah—the whale couldn't keep him down.

Sunday school teacher: What do you think the
"land flowing with milk and honey" will be like?
Student: Sticky!

What is the strongest day in the week?
Sunday. The rest are weekdays.

Which came first, the chicken or the egg?
The chicken, of course. God doesn't lay eggs.

Do you know what the name of Isaiah's horse was?
"Is Me." Isaiah said, "Woe, is me."

Baseball is talked about a great deal in the Bible:

In the big inning.
Eve stole first.

Adam stole second.
Gideon rattled the pitchers.
Goliath was put out by David.
The prodigal son made a home run.

At what season did Eve eat the fruit?
Early in the fall.

What did Adam first plant in the Garden of Eden?
His foot.

What did Adam never see or possess, yet left two
  for each of his children?
Parents.

How were Adam and Eve prevented from gam-
  bling?
Their paradise (pair-o-dice) was taken away from them.

Bill: What was Eve's telephone number in the
  Garden of Eden?
Jill: I think it was Adam-812.

Where is deviled ham mentioned in the Bible?
When the evil spirits entered the swine.

★ ★ ★

Even Adam and Eve had their problems. One day Adam got angry.

"You've done it again, Eve," said Adam. "You put my shirt in the salad again."

44

The Chopping Block

Do you know of any cures for insomnia?
Try talking to yourself.

I'm chilled to the bone.
Why don't you put on your hat?

I have a bitter taste in my mouth.
Been biting your tongue?

George: And what makes you think he deserves
the name Great Lover?
Chris: I watched him standing before a mirror.

Bill: I have had to make a living by my wits.
Gill: Well, half a living is better than none.

Kim: And what brings you to town?
Shana: I just came to see the sights, and I thought
  I'd call on you first.

Peg: Something came into my mind just now and
  went away again.
LaRae: Maybe it was lonely.

Julie: That singer has a terrible voice. Do you know
  who she is?
Carolyn: Yes, she is my sister.
Julie: Well, I really didn't mean her voice, it is the
  music she has to sing. I wonder who wrote that
  awful music.
Carolyn: I did.

Him: When I stand on my head, the blood rushes
  to it. Why doesn't it rush to my feet when I
  stand up?
Her: Because your feet aren't empty.

Betty: You should be ashamed of yourself,
  laughing at that fat man.
Barb: I'm just having fun at his expanse.

★ ★ ★

Mary: My husband had my photograph over his heart during the war. In fact, it stopped a bullet one time and saved his life.

Jerri: I'm not surprised, dear. It would stop anything.

Hokum: What do you mean by telling everyone I am deaf and dumb?

Yokum: That's not true. I never said you were deaf.

James: You say there was something in her speech that sounded strange. What was that?

Keith: A pause.

She: You remind me of Don Juan.

He (flattered): Tell me how.

She: Well, for one thing, he's been dead for years.

Him: I am a self-made man!

Her: Why did you make yourself like that?

Jack: I suppose you think I'm a perfect idiot.

Jean: Oh, none of us is perfect.

Terry: I simply can't bear idiots!
Steve: How odd...apparently your mother could.

Rob: This oil makes my leg smart.
Joy: Try rubbing it on your head.

Nadine: My opinion of you is a perfectly
  contemptible one.
Susie: I never knew any opinion of yours that was
  not contemptible.

Paul: I am a self-made man!
Lou: Well, that relieves the Almighty of a great
  responsibility.

Henry: I believe I could write like Shakespeare if I
  had a mind to try it.
Charlie: Yes, nothing is wanting but the mind!

Pete: Our dog is just like one of the family.
Nancy: Really? Which one?

Katie: Everyone says I got my good looks from my father.
Donna: Is he a plastic surgeon?

Peggy: I got a job working for a drugstore. I'm supposed to increase business.
Linda: What do you do? Stand out front and make people sick?

Jim: Has anyone ever told you how wonderful you are?
Georgia: Nope.
Jim: Then where did you get the idea?

Lori: I can't catch my breath!
Kerri: With your breath you should be thankful!

Paula: Not very funny, is he?
Henri: No, he couldn't even entertain a doubt.

Susan: You know, you've changed since I saw you last.
Kari: For better or worse?
Susan: You could only change for the better.

Matt: I'm a lady killer.
Terri: Yeah, they take one look at you and drop dead.

Pam: I've been asked to get married lots of times.
Dana: Who asked you?
Pam: Mother and father.

Lori: I read your new book yesterday. I loved it. Who wrote it for you?
Kay: I'm glad you liked it. Who read it to you?

Wanda: And when I was 16, the president of the United States presented a beauty award to me.
Renee: Really? I didn't think President Lincoln bothered with that sort of thing!

Ruth: How do you like it? It's just a little something I threw on.
David: Looks like you missed.

Samson: What happened to that dopey blonde Mike used to run around with?
Naomi: I dyed my hair!

Girl: You remind me of an ocean.
Boy: You mean wild, restless, and romantic?
Girl: No, you just make me sick.

Debra: A lot of guys are going to be miserable
when I marry.
Priscilla: Really? How many are you going to
marry?

DJ: I'm homesick!
Mike: But you're at home!
DJ: I know…and I'm sick of it!

At a supermarket a woman crowded ahead of
another shopper.
"I hope you don't mind," said the woman who
was carrying a can. "All I wanted was this cat
food."
"Not at all," replied the other coolly. "You look
hungry."

★ ★ ★

First soldier: I'd let those doctors experiment on
me for the sake of science. I'm not afraid. I've
gone through the war. Why I even once volun-
teered to let them put a new heart into my chest
if one was available which suited my character.

Second soldier: What was the matter? Couldn't
 they find a chicken big enough?

LaVon: This lace is over 60 years old.
Sylvia: Really? Over 60 years old? Did you make it
 yourself?

Arnold: The president has personally asked me
 to help beautify the United States on a special
 project.
Tommy: Really? Which country have you decided
 to move to?

Nina: Sam says I look like a million!
Christy: Yeah, all wrinkled and green.

She: Whenever some bore at a party asks me what
 I do for a living I say I'm a juggler with a circus.
He: And what do you do for a living?
She: I'm a juggler with a circus!

Charlie: I wish I had been born in the Dark Ages.
George: So do I. You look terrible in the light.

Kelly: What do you call frozen water?
Kim: Iced water.
Kelly: What do you call frozen ink?
Kim: Iced ink.
Kelly: You're telling me!

Rick: Well, I must be going.
Natalie: Don't let me keep you if you really must
 be going.
Rick: Yes, I really must go. But, really, I did enjoy
 our little visit. Do you know, when I came in
 here I had a headache but now I have lost it
 entirely.
Natalie: Oh, it isn't lost. I've got it now.

A tired guest at a party spoke to the boy next to
 him.
"Gee, this thing is a bore; I'm going to beat it!"
"I would, too," said the boy, "but I've got to stay.
 It's my house!"

Anita: Don't bother showing me to the door.
Sam: It's no bother...it's a pleasure!

Joy: You're not smart enough to talk to an idiot!
Marian: Okay. I'll send you a letter.

Charlotte: Thank goodness that misery is over!
Georgia: What misery?
Charlotte: Talking with the host. Have you been
　　through it yet?
Georgia: I don't have to. I'm the host's girlfriend!

Debbie: When I got on the bus three men got up to
　　give me their seats.
Holly: Did you take them?

Dali: Is this one of your silly abstract paintings?
Pablo: No, that's a mirror!

Mary: I don't look 16, do I?
Martha: Not anymore!

Kyle: Did you see that young lady smile at me?
Kerri: That's nothing. The first time I saw you, I
　　laughed out loud.

James: I kissed her under the mistletoe.
Keith: I wouldn't kiss her under anesthetic!

Chris: How dare you belch before my date!
Bob: Sorry, ol' pal. I didn't know it was her turn!

Clara: My boyfriend says I look younger in this
   hat.
Sara: Oh, really? What is your age?
Clara. Sixteen.
Sara: No, I mean without the hat!

Donna: Is it raining outside?
Kathie: Have you ever seen it rain inside?

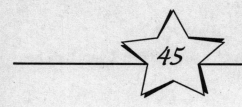

Zingy Zingers

Why don't you sue your brains for nonsupport?

He has a small birthmark on his head...his brain.

When he meets another egotist, it's an I for an I.

You're really old you if you can remember when a family went for a Sunday drive—and everyone got in the same car.

"Mommy, before you married Daddy, who told you how to drive?"

He was so ugly when he was a baby they used to diaper his face.

My brother is on a seafood diet. Every time he sees food, he eats.

We've just moved into our dream house. It costs twice as much as we ever dreamed it would.

Is that your face or did your neck throw up?

We had such a bad team that every time we took the field our manager got fined for littering.

I once prayed in a hotel, and they charged me a 75-cent long-distance charge.

Crime is so bad in my neighborhood we have the only police station in town that's insured against burglary.

Sign at a traffic court: Don't complain. Think of the tickets you deserved but didn't get!

Anyone who goes to a psychiatrist ought to have his head examined.

He's the kind of guy that can really creep into your heart and mind.
In fact, you'll never meet a bigger creep!

She has delusions of glamour.

A garage sale is a technique for distributing all the junk in your garage among all the other garages in the neighborhood.

Her idea of housework is to sweep the room with a glance.

My mother had a terrible accident in the kitchen the other night...and we had to eat it!

He is the kind of guy that would go to a home for the blind and pound the Braille flat.

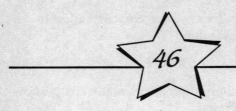

Dating Game

He: Here is your engagement ring.
She: But this diamond has a flaw in it.
He: You shouldn't notice that…we are in love and love is blind.
She: Not stone blind.

Father: How dare you! What do you mean by hugging my daughter?
Boy: I–I–I was just carrying out the scriptural injunction "hold fast that which is good."

Her: Will you love me when I am old?
He: I will love you. I will cherish the ground you walk upon. I will…you won't look like your mother, will you?

"Bill told me I was the only girl he ever loved."
"Doesn't he say it beautifully?"

He: If you would give me your phone number I would give you a call.
She: It's in the book.
He: Good. What's your name?
She: It's in the book, too.

After a Dutch-treat-on-everything date, the girl responded to her escort who brought her home, "Since we've gone Dutch on everything else, you can just kiss yourself goodnight!"

He: Will you marry me?
She: No.
And they lived happily ever after.

Him: If I tried to kiss you, would you call for help?
Her: Do you need help?

Jean: When are you thinking about getting married?
Joan: Constantly.

"If you refuse to marry me I will die," said the young romantic. And, sure enough, 50 years later he did.

Girl: Would you like to take a walk?
Boy: I'd love to.
Girl: Well, don't let me keep you.

"She thinks no man is good enough for her."
"She may be right."
"She may be left."

Conceited: I can tell just by looking into a girl's eyes exactly how she feels about me.
Girl: Gee, that must be embarrassing for you.

Him: There is one word that will make me the happiest man in the world. Will you marry me?
Her: No.
Him: That's the word!

★ ★ ★

Bill: I think I'm in love.
Pete: Really?
Bill: Yes. All I need to do is find a girl.

Boy: I guess you've been out with worse looking
fellows than I am, haven't you?

Boy: ...I guess you've been out with worse looking
fellows than I am, haven't you?

Girl: I heard you the first time. I was thinking.

Boy: I want to be honest. You're not the first girl
I've kissed.

Girl: I want to be honest. You've got a lot to learn.

★ ★ ★

Boy: You could learn to love me, couldn't you?

Girl: Well, I learned to eat spinach.

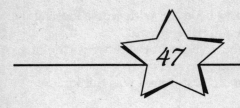

Food for Thought

Customer: I am sorry, waiter, but I only have enough money for the bill. I have nothing left for a tip:

Waiter: Let me add up that bill again, sir.

Customer: One of the claws on this lobster is missing.

Waiter: They fight in the kitchen and sometimes bite each other's claws off.

Customer: Then take this one back and bring me a winner.

Waiter: We have a very up-to-date place here. Everything is cooked by electricity.

Customer: I wonder if you would mind giving this steak another shock?

Customer: Would you mind taking the fly out of my soup?
Waiter: Do it yourself. I'm no lifeguard.

Customer: This coffee tastes like mud.
Waiter: Well, it was ground this morning.

Man: There's a splinter in my cottage cheese!
Waiter: What do you expect for 55 cents...the whole cottage?

Eat, drink and be merry for tomorrow we diet.

Some people are no good at counting calories, and they have the figures to prove it.

A man took his ten-year-old son to an elegant restaurant and was surprised to hear him order the usual hamburger.

"Try something different and unusual," he urged him.

"I am," he whispered. "I've never had a ten-dollar hamburger before!"

Help! Police!

Robber: I'm going to shoot you.
Man: Why?
Robber: I shoot anyone who looks like me.
Man: Do I look like you?
Robber: Yes.
Man: Then shoot!

Judge: Haven't I seen you before?
Man: Yes, Your Honor. I taught your daughter how to play the piano.
Judge: Thirty years.

Judge: What good have you ever done for society?
Robber: Well, I've kept four or five detectives working regularly.

★ ★ ★

Police officer: In the gun battle a bullet struck my head and went into space.
Doctor: Well, at least you're honest.

Speeder: But, Judge, I do everything fast.
Judge: Let's see how fast you can do 30 days.

Police officer: Name, please.
Motorist: Wilhem Von Corquerinski Popolavawitz.
Police officer: Well...don't let me catch you speeding again.

Robber: Give me all your money.
Citizen: All I have is a watch, and it only has sentimental value.
Robber: Fork it over. I feel like a good cry.

Judge: Thirty years in prison!
Prisoner: But, Judge, I won't live that long!
Judge: Just do what you can.

★ ★ ★

Things are getting so bad in my neighborhood that one gangster does all his holdups in daylight. He's afraid to be out on the street at night with all that money.

Other Books by Bob Phillips

For information on how to purchase any of the above books, contact your
local bookstore or send a self-addressed stamped envelope to:
Family Services
P.O.Box 9363
Fresno, CA 93702